INDESTRUCTIBLE NATURE OF

TARDIGRADES

The Secrets behind the Indestructible Nature and Everything You need to Know about Tardigrades

JOHNNY MAX CARSON

This BOOK belongs to

____

____

From:

____

Signature/Date:

____

TABLE OF CONTENTS

INTRODUCTION

Tardigrades, often whimsically referred to as "water bears," have long captured the fascination of scientists and laypeople alike with their extraordinary resilience in the face of extreme conditions.

From the vacuum of space to the depths of the ocean floor, these microscopic creatures have demonstrated an unparalleled ability to survive and thrive in environments that would prove fatal to most other organisms. In recent years, research efforts have intensified in an attempt to unravel the mysteries behind tardigrade resilience, leading to groundbreaking discoveries that could revolutionize our understanding of biology, medicine, and material science.

In this comprehensive exploration, we delve into the latest findings surrounding tardigrade resilience, examine the underlying mechanisms driving their remarkable survival capabilities, and explore the wide-ranging implications for science and technology.

CHAPTER 1

THE INCREDIBLE WORLD OF TARDIGRADES

Tardigrades, often affectionately referred to as "water bears," are microscopic organisms that belong to the phylum Tardigrada. Despite their diminutive size, tardigrades have captured the imagination of scientists and enthusiasts alike due to their remarkable resilience and ability to survive in some of the most extreme environments on Earth and beyond.

1.1. Introduction to Tardigrades

Tardigrades were first discovered by the German zoologist Johann August Ephraim Goeze in 1773, who initially described them as "little water bears" due to their bear-like appearance and aquatic habitat. These fascinating creatures typically measure between 0.1 to 1.5 millimeters in length and are found in diverse ecosystems worldwide, including terrestrial habitats such as mosses, lichens, soil, and leaf litter, as well as aquatic environments like freshwater and marine ecosystems.

Despite their small size, tardigrades exhibit a remarkable diversity of forms, with over 1,300 species described to date. Their body structure consists of four pairs of stubby legs, each equipped with claws or suction cups for locomotion. Tardigrades also possess a distinctive barrel-shaped body and a mouth equipped with piercing stylets used for feeding on plant cells, algae, and small invertebrates.

1.2. Extreme Environments

One of the most captivating aspects of tardigrades is their ability to thrive in environments that would be considered inhospitable or lethal to most other organisms. From the scorching deserts of Antarctica to the depths of the Mariana Trench, tardigrades have been found in virtually every habitat on Earth. They can withstand extreme temperatures ranging from near absolute zero (-273 degrees Celsius) to over 150 degrees Celsius, as well as pressures exceeding 1,000 times that of Earth's atmosphere.

Tardigrades are also highly resilient to desiccation, or extreme dryness, which allows them to survive in environments with low water availability. In fact, tardigrades can enter a state of cryptobiosis, where they effectively shut down their metabolism and become dormant until conditions improve. This remarkable survival strategy, known as the "tun state," enables tardigrades to survive for years or even decades without water.

1.3. Tardigrade Resilience

The resilience of tardigrades extends beyond their ability to withstand extreme temperatures, pressures, and desiccation. These hardy organisms have also demonstrated remarkable tolerance to radiation, exposure to toxins, and even the vacuum of space. Studies have shown that tardigrades exposed to high doses of radiation or placed in the vacuum of space can survive and reproduce, further highlighting their extraordinary adaptability.

One of the most intriguing aspects of tardigrade resilience is their ability to repair DNA damage caused by environmental stressors. Tardigrades possess unique DNA repair mechanisms that allow them to fix double-strand breaks and other types of damage more efficiently than other organisms. This exceptional DNA repair capacity may contribute to their ability to survive in harsh environments where DNA damage is common.

1.4. Historical Perspective

The study of tardigrades dates back to the late 18th century when Goeze first described these enigmatic creatures. Since then, researchers have made significant strides in understanding tardigrade biology, ecology, and resilience. Early studies focused on describing tardigrade morphology and taxonomy, laying the groundwork for subsequent research into their remarkable survival abilities.

In recent decades, advances in microscopy, molecular biology, and genomic sequencing have enabled scientists to delve deeper into the mechanisms underlying tardigrade resilience. From the identification of stress-induced proteins and protective molecules to the characterization of genetic pathways involved in cryptobiosis, researchers have made significant progress in unraveling the secrets of tardigrade survival.

Overall, the study of tardigrades continues to inspire awe and curiosity among scientists and enthusiasts alike. These resilient creatures offer valuable insights into the limits of life on Earth and the potential for survival in extreme environments. As research into tardigrade biology advances, we gain a deeper appreciation for the wonders of the natural world and the incredible adaptations that enable life to thrive in the most unlikely places.

CHAPTER 2

DECODING TARDIGRADE RESILIENCE

Tardigrades, with their ability to survive extreme conditions, have long fascinated scientists. In this chapter, we delve into the mechanisms behind their resilience, exploring the intricate processes that enable these tiny organisms to endure harsh environments and enter a state of suspended animation known as the tun state.

2.1. The Tun State

At the heart of tardigrade resilience lies the remarkable phenomenon known as the tun state. When faced with adverse conditions such as desiccation, extreme temperatures, or high levels of radiation, tardigrades enter a state of suspended animation where metabolic activity is drastically reduced. In this dormant state, tardigrades curl up into a ball-like shape, retracting their eight legs and minimizing water loss. This adaptive response allows tardigrades to survive for extended periods without food or water, waiting for more favorable conditions to return.

The tun state is characterized by a cessation of most metabolic processes, including respiration, digestion, and reproduction. Instead, tardigrades rely on energy reserves stored within their bodies to sustain them during periods of dormancy. This remarkable ability to enter a state of suspended animation enables tardigrades to survive in environments that would be lethal to most other organisms, making them true masters of survival.

2.2. Oxidative Stress and Reactive Oxygen Species

While the tun state provides tardigrades with a powerful defense against environmental stressors, the mechanisms underlying this resilience have long remained a mystery. Recent research has shed light on the role of oxidative stress and reactive oxygen species (ROS) in triggering the tun state. Oxidative stress occurs when the balance between the production of ROS and the antioxidant defenses of an organism is disrupted, leading to cellular damage and dysfunction.

In tardigrades, exposure to extreme conditions such as desiccation or radiation results in the production of ROS within their cells. These highly reactive molecules can damage proteins, DNA, and other cellular components if left unchecked. However, tardigrades possess robust antioxidant defenses that help neutralize ROS and mitigate their harmful effects. By regulating the balance of ROS within their cells, tardigrades are able to activate the protective mechanisms that lead to the tun state.

2.3. Cysteines as Signaling Molecules

Central to the activation of the tun state are cysteines, a type of amino acid found in tardigrade proteins. Research has revealed that cysteines play a crucial role in signaling the onset of the protective mechanisms that lead to the tun state. When exposed to ROS, cysteines undergo a process known as oxidation, where they form disulfide bonds with other cysteine molecules. This oxidative modification serves as a signal to the tardigrade's cells that environmental conditions are becoming unfavorable, prompting them to enter the tun state as a protective measure.

The discovery of cysteines as signaling molecules represents a significant breakthrough in our understanding of tardigrade resilience. By elucidating the molecular mechanisms underlying the activation of the tun state, researchers have gained valuable insights into how tardigrades are able to survive in extreme environments and endure prolonged periods of stress.

2.4. Experimental Approaches

The study of tardigrade resilience relies on a combination of experimental approaches, including microscopy, genetic analysis, and environmental stress tests. Microscopy techniques such as scanning electron microscopy (SEM) and transmission electron microscopy (TEM) allow researchers to visualize the ultrastructure of tardigrade cells and tissues with high resolution. This enables them to study the effects of environmental stressors on cellular morphology and identify key adaptations that contribute to tardigrade resilience.

Genetic analysis techniques such as RNA sequencing and CRISPR-Cas9 gene editing have provided valuable insights into the genetic pathways involved in tardigrade resilience. By identifying genes that are upregulated or downregulated in response to environmental stressors, researchers can uncover the molecular mechanisms underlying the activation of the tun state and other protective mechanisms.

Environmental stress tests involve exposing tardigrades to controlled conditions such as desiccation, extreme temperatures, or radiation, and monitoring their physiological responses. By subjecting tardigrades to various stressors and observing their behavior, researchers can gain insights into the adaptive strategies employed by these resilient organisms to survive in harsh environments.

The mechanisms underlying tardigrade resilience are multifaceted and complex, involving a delicate balance of oxidative stress, antioxidant defenses, and molecular signaling pathways. By unraveling these intricacies, scientists are not only gaining a deeper understanding of tardigrade biology but also uncovering valuable insights into the broader principles of stress tolerance and survival in living organisms.

CHAPTER 3

IMPLICATIONS FOR HUMAN HEALTH

Tardigrades, with their remarkable resilience and ability to survive extreme conditions, hold immense potential for applications in human health. In this chapter, we explore how insights from tardigrade research could inform the development of novel medical therapies, bioinspired technologies, and biomedical engineering solutions, with a focus on cancer treatment, drug discovery, and biomedical engineering.

3.1. Medical Applications

One of the most promising areas of research stemming from tardigrade resilience is the development of novel medical therapies. Tardigrades possess unique adaptations that enable them to survive in harsh environments, including the ability to repair DNA damage and withstand extreme temperatures and pressures. These adaptations could hold the key to developing new treatments for diseases such as cancer, where resistance to chemotherapy and radiation therapy remains a major challenge.

By studying the mechanisms underlying tardigrade resilience, researchers hope to identify new targets for cancer therapy and develop strategies to enhance the effectiveness of existing treatments. For example, insights into tardigrade DNA repair mechanisms could lead to the development of novel drugs that sensitize cancer cells to chemotherapy or radiation therapy, making them more susceptible to treatment.

Additionally, the ability of tardigrades to enter a state of suspended animation in response to environmental stressors could inspire new approaches to preserving organs for transplantation. By harnessing the principles of tardigrade resilience, researchers could develop techniques to prolong the viability of organs outside the body, reducing the risk of organ rejection and increasing the availability of donor organs for patients in need.

3.2. Bioinspired Technologies

In addition to medical applications, tardigrade resilience has inspired the development of bioinspired technologies for a wide range of applications. One area of particular interest is the development of protective materials for use in extreme environments, such as space exploration and firefighting. Tardigrades are able to survive in the vacuum of space and withstand extreme temperatures and pressures, making them ideal candidates for biomimetic materials that can protect humans and equipment in hostile environments.

Researchers are also exploring the use of tardigrade-inspired materials for medical applications, such as wound dressings and implants. By mimicking the structure and properties of tardigrade cuticles, researchers hope to develop materials that are both biocompatible and durable, making them ideal for use in medical devices and implants.

3.3. Drug Discovery

Another area of research with significant potential stemming from tardigrade resilience is drug discovery. Tardigrades produce a variety of unique compounds that enable them to survive in harsh environments, some of which may have therapeutic properties for human health. By studying the molecules produced by tardigrades and their effects on cellular processes, researchers hope to identify new drug candidates for the treatment of a wide range of diseases.

For example, tardigrades produce proteins and peptides that protect their cells from damage caused by environmental stressors, such as desiccation and radiation. These molecules could serve as inspiration for the development of new drugs that protect human cells from similar types of damage, making them more resilient to disease and aging.

3.4. Biomedical Engineering

Finally, tardigrade resilience has implications for biomedical engineering, particularly in the development of tissue engineering and regenerative medicine solutions. Tardigrades possess unique adaptations that enable them to survive in harsh environments and repair damage to their cells and tissues. By studying the mechanisms underlying tardigrade resilience, researchers hope to develop new approaches to tissue regeneration and organ repair that could revolutionize the field of regenerative medicine.

For example, insights into tardigrade DNA repair mechanisms could inspire new strategies for repairing damaged tissues and organs in humans. By mimicking the molecular pathways and mechanisms used by tardigrades to repair DNA damage, researchers could develop new techniques for regenerating damaged tissues and organs, offering new hope for patients suffering from injuries and degenerative diseases.

Tardigrade resilience holds immense potential for applications in human health, including the development of novel medical therapies, bioinspired technologies, and biomedical engineering solutions. By unraveling the secrets of tardigrade resilience, researchers are paving the way for new treatments and technologies that could improve the lives of millions of people around the world.

CHAPTER 4

FUTURE DIRECTIONS AND CHALLENGES

As research into tardigrade resilience continues to advance, exciting opportunities and challenges lie ahead. In this chapter, we explore the future directions of tardigrade research, identify key unanswered questions, discuss emerging technologies, and address ethical considerations surrounding the study of these fascinating organisms.

4.1. Unanswered Questions

Despite significant progress in understanding tardigrade resilience, numerous unanswered questions remain. One key area of interest is the molecular mechanisms underlying the tun state and how tardigrades are able to enter and exit this state with such precision. Additionally, researchers are still working to fully elucidate the role of oxidative stress and reactive oxygen species in triggering the protective mechanisms that lead to the tun state.

Another unanswered question relates to the genetic basis of tardigrade resilience. While recent studies have identified genes and pathways associated with stress tolerance and survival, much remains to be discovered about the genetic mechanisms that enable tardigrades to thrive in extreme environments. Furthermore, the role of epigenetic factors and non-coding RNAs in regulating tardigrade resilience warrants further investigation.

4.2. Technological Innovation

Advances in technology are expected to accelerate progress in tardigrade research, enabling researchers to tackle complex questions with unprecedented precision and efficiency. One area of particular promise is the development of advanced imaging techniques that allow researchers to visualize tardigrade cells and tissues with high resolution. Techniques such as cryo-electron microscopy and super-resolution microscopy are providing new insights into the ultrastructure of tardigrade cells and the molecular mechanisms underlying their resilience.

Genomic sequencing technologies are also driving progress in tardigrade research, enabling researchers to sequence the genomes of tardigrade species and identify genes associated with stress tolerance and survival. Additionally, emerging technologies such as single-cell RNA sequencing and CRISPR-based gene editing are revolutionizing our ability to study gene expression and function in tardigrades, opening up new avenues for research into their biology and resilience.

4.3. Ethical Considerations

As research into tardigrade resilience advances, it is important to consider the ethical implications of studying these organisms. Tardigrades are living organisms with complex biological systems, and ethical considerations surrounding their use in research must be carefully considered. Researchers must ensure that their studies adhere to ethical guidelines and principles, including the principles of replacement, refinement, and reduction in animal research.

Furthermore, researchers must consider the potential environmental impact of their studies, particularly when conducting experiments that involve the manipulation or introduction of tardigrades into new environments. Tardigrades play important roles in ecosystems worldwide, and researchers must take care to minimize any potential harm to these organisms and their habitats.

4.4. Collaborative Efforts

Collaboration and interdisciplinary research will be key to advancing our understanding of tardigrade resilience and translating research findings into practical applications. By bringing together experts from diverse fields, including biology, chemistry, physics, engineering, and medicine, researchers can leverage their collective expertise to tackle complex questions and develop innovative solutions.

International collaboration will also be crucial, as tardigrades are found in diverse habitats around the world, and research efforts must be coordinated to ensure that all species and ecosystems are adequately represented. By fostering collaboration and sharing resources and data, researchers can accelerate progress in tardigrade research and maximize the potential for scientific discovery and innovation.

The future of tardigrade research holds immense promise, with exciting opportunities for scientific discovery and technological innovation. By addressing key unanswered questions, leveraging emerging technologies, and considering ethical considerations, researchers can unlock the full potential of tardigrade resilience and harness it for the benefit of humanity and the natural world.

CONCLUSION

The study of tardigrade resilience represents a captivating frontier of scientific inquiry with far-reaching implications for diverse fields, including biology, medicine, material science, and engineering. These extraordinary organisms, with their ability to survive in extreme environments and enter a state of suspended animation known as the tun state, have captivated the imagination of researchers and enthusiasts alike.

Through meticulous research and experimentation, scientists have begun to unravel the secrets of tardigrade resilience, uncovering the molecular mechanisms that underlie their remarkable survival abilities. Insights into oxidative stress, reactive oxygen species, and molecular signaling pathways have shed light on how tardigrades withstand environmental stressors and thrive in hostile conditions.

The implications of tardigrade research are profound and multifaceted. From the development of novel medical therapies and bioinspired technologies to advancements in drug discovery and biomedical engineering, tardigrade resilience holds immense potential for improving human health and addressing some of the most important issues confronting civilization.

As research into tardigrade resilience continues to advance, it is essential to address key unanswered questions, leverage emerging technologies, and consider ethical considerations surrounding the study of these fascinating organisms. By fostering collaboration and interdisciplinary research efforts, scientists can unlock the full potential of tardigrade resilience and harness it for the betterment of humanity and the natural world.

In essence, the study of tardigrades exemplifies the awe-inspiring complexity and resilience of life on Earth, offering valuable insights into the limits of survival and the potential for adaptation in the face of adversity. As we continue to explore the mysteries of these extraordinary creatures, we embark on a journey of discovery that promises to transform our understanding of biology and inspire new innovations for generations to come.